A Journey Through India

A Journey Through India

TIGER BOOKS INTERNATIONAL
LONDON

PHOTOCREDITS

(Page numbers)

Raghu Rai
Cover, 26-27

Gurmeet Thukral
7, 31, 42-43, 48, 49, 54-55, 56, 57, 58, 59, 60, 61, 62-63, 66, 67, 72-73,
74-75, 86, 87, 90-91, 92, 93

D.N. Dube
2, 7, 29, 32-33, 34-35, 36, 37, 40, 41, 64-65, 70, 71, 77, 86, 88, 89

P. Kapoor
3, 7, 28, 30, 38, 39, 40, 45, 50-51, 66, 68, 80-81, 82, 83

J.L. Nou
2, 3, 76, 77, 78, 79, 94-95, 96

Sondeep Shankar
30, 31, 46, 47

| **M.D. Sharma** | **Ashok Khanna** | **Aditya Patankar** |
| 7, 44, 46 | 3, 7, 69 | 52-53 |

| **P.N. Ahuja** | **Rajesh Bedi** | **Raghubir Singh** |
| 84-85 | 69 | 48 |

Text by Supriya Guha

First published in India 1984
Revised edition 1986 by
Lustre Press Pvt. Ltd.,
5 Ansari Road, Daryaganj,
New Delhi, India

Reprinted in 1990

This edition published by
Tiger Books International Ltd.
3 Friars Lane, Richmond,
Surrey TW9 1NL
U.K.

ISBN 1-870461-41-X

Printed and bound by Toppan Printing Co. (S) Pte. Ltd., Singapore

ULTIMATELY, YOU will have to drive every banal image from your mind. Every cliche from newspapers and books, television and the cinema will prove to be a fractional truth. For India cannot be fitted into a readymade slot. The India of the Raj, submerged in a mire of vicarious nostalgia; the India of the curmudgeon travel writer—decadent, corrupt, and quite, quite hopeless; the Hippie Haven—the hard sell of the sixties; it will not do. You will have to erase all these stereotypes, and then you may discover your own India; for there is not just one India but many that coexist and sometimes overlap and merge into one another in a bewildering montage.

The tourist brochure proclaims, India is a land of startling contrasts. And the government handbook trots out the catchphrase, 'Unity in Diversity'. All of which is trite but true. Centuries of invasions and migrations and the consequent mingling of peoples have resulted in a great variety of physical types. The palette of Indian skin tones ranges from pale to swarthy, while facial features display tremendous diversity. The people of India speak one or more of fifteen different languages and over 200 dialects; they may be Hindus, Muslims, Sikhs, Buddhists, Christians, Zoroastrians or Jews. What, then, in this Babel of tongues and ways of worship, ultimately binds the Indian people together? The idea of India has roots that go deeper in the popular mind than regional or sectarian loyalties. At the more quotidian level, the rhythm of the seasons with its impact on life and work, local cults and beliefs has bound rural life in a common thread. In the cities the compulsions of industry and urban life have led to a new logic, a new impetus that holds diverse groups together in a sense of community. Both the contrasts and the continuity are a product of India's varied topography and long history.

Academic fashion prefers the term South Asia now, but with its geographical, ethnic and linguistic multiplicity India is best described as a subcontinent. The northern ramparts of the Himalayas and the moat made up of three seas washing peninsular India's long coastline have in a sense kept India distinct from adjacent geographical or cultural regions. The Himalayas served as a barrier against the icy winds of Central Asia, but were not always affective against political intruders. From the north-western passes came the Aryan horsemen who settled down and gave Indian society and culture much of its character. Later came the Greeks, the Scythians, the Parthians, the Turks and Afghans and others—including, of course, the Mughals. Navigators, too, succeeded in crossing the oceans to reach

The many faces of India: The characteristic diversity of skin tones and physical features found among Indians is a consequence of centuries of invasions, migrations and mingling of peoples.

the coveted treasure trove of India. From before the Christian era, the coast saw foreign sailors—Romans and, later, Arabs—whose trading settlements linked India with the world. It was by sea, again, that Indian arts and religious ideas spread to South-East Asia—to Indonesia, Indochina and Thailand. In brief, India's natural boundaries kept her aloof enough to retain and develop a distinct identity, but never completely cut off or isolated her from the world beyond.

The Himalayas are the highest mountain range in the world—and considered by many to be the most spectacular. Long sanctified in the Hindu tradition as the abode of the gods, they are dotted with venerated places of pilgrimage. The splendour of their snowy summits, icy lakes, deep forests and rocky fastnesses has for ages lured the mystic and the explorer.

The Himalayas are also the source of some of the mightiest rivers of India, fed by glaciers and melting snows, swelling and changing colour with each confluence, growing wide and ponderous in the plains. The Indus, from which India and Hinduism derive their names, is fed by five major tributaries that flow southwards from the mountains, giving the area the name of Punjab—the land of five rivers. The Gangetic plain extends from the foothills of the Himalayas to the Bay of Bengal but the spiritual power of the river Ganga itself resonates over a far wider territory. Every *prayag* or confluence in the hills where the Ganga is augmented by a tributary is a sacred place and all along the course of the river pilgrims bathe in the holy water. The major *teerthasthanas* or places of pilgrimage of North India are associated with the Ganga—Hardwar, Allahabad and the holiest of holies, Banaras.

The Ganga is revered as a goddess, like her sister Parvati, daughter of the mountains and consort of the god Shiva. The Ganga is called Mother and the lands through which she does not flow are seen as bereft and desolate. The 11th century South Indian king Rajaraja Chola carried home Ganga water after a successful campaign in the north and mixed it with the waters of the Kaveri. And to celebrate this auspicious occasion, he built a new city called Gangai-kondacholapuram—'the city of the Chola conqueror of the Ganga'.

The Gangetic plain was the birthplace of Buddhism. As one travels through the vast agricultural expanse, the Buddha's evocative description of the garments of the ascetic *bhikshu* or monk—'patched like the fields of Magadha'—comes to mind as shades of brown and green alternate. Further eastwards, the green begins to dominate, interrupted by cities ancient and new, the final one being the largest and most densely populated city of India—Calcutta, situated in the Gangetic delta.

The north-eastern wing of India is watered by the third mighty river of the north, the Brahmaputra. The tropical forests of this region are rich in a variety of orchids, spices and timber, and the wet, grassy lowlands of Assam are the last remaining home of the Indian one-horned rhinoceros. The foothills of this extension of the Himalayas get the heaviest rainfall from the monsoon, the moisture-laden wind that brings rain to much of India and chiefly determines its climatic patterns. Over most of India, in fact, the monsoons regulate the rhythm of life—the crops and the harvests and, consequently, the seasons of labour and days of festivity. The same monsoon wind is nearly depleted by the time it reaches Rajasthan in Western India, which lies outside both the Indus valley and the Gangetic plain. Nature has thus given India an area with a spectacular desert landscape, with flat sandy stretches broken by the Aravalli hills that create patches of green forest and innumerable small lakes.

Peninsular India is geologically the oldest part of the subcontinent. Most of it is a rocky plateau, flanked by hills that make up the Western and Eastern Ghats. Between the Ghats and the sea lie coastal plains. The rocky landscapes of the Deccan plateau strike a startling contrast to the green coastal belts. The Malabar coast on the west is narrower than the eastern or Coromandel coast and has some luxuriant palm-lined beaches—the famous Goa beaches, for example, and the spectacular beach at Kovalam in Kerala.

Nature is varied and diverse and so are the ways in which people have coped with her, used her and learnt to live with her. This is reflected in a myriad ways in India—in the use of locally available materials for houses, in the clothes people wear, in the way they live and work, worship and celebrate. Every region and locality has its own traditions and customs traversing the many cross-cutting loyalties of religion, community and caste. Yet the idea of India as one land is ancient and deeply rooted in the Indian consciousness. The democratic republic of the twentieth century may well have been fashioned on the Western idea of the nation-state. But the *char dham* or four sacred sites have been located in the four corners of the country and visited by pilgrims from all over India for centuries.

Ancient India

TO MOST READERS, Indian history appears a bewildering succession of kings and empires, battles and struggles. At the end, it may be hard to imagine how, during the most turbulent periods, the everyday ways of life and ritual, of the arts and of folklore managed to survive and be passed down. It was in fact the resilience of custom and popular tradition which transcended all the cataclysms of politics and enabled a cultural continuity, even as changes occurred and were absorbed. Viewed very broadly, patterns can be seen in the evolution of Indian society that go back at least as far as some 3,500 years.

The discovery of an ancient civilization, concentrated around the river valley of the Indus but spreading far beyond to the east and south-east, was one of the most exciting events in the study of Indian history. The cities of Harappa and Mohenjo-Daro (now in Pakistan), Kalibangan (Rajasthan), Lothal (Gujarat) and other sites showed that Indian civilization was as old as the Chinese, Mesopotamian and Egyptian civilizations. The script of the Indus civilization has not been conclusively deciphered, but the cities show a remarkable level of sophistication in town-planning, the use of burnt bricks in construction and a central system of drainage.

The Aryans who took over the northern parts of India came from Afghanistan and Iran, though their original home was probably in the steppes of Central Asia. A nomadic, pastoral people whose society was organized on tribal lines, the Aryans saw cattle as their chief wealth; the veneration given to the cow in India even today can be traced to early Vedic times.

The period of the Aryan settlement along the Ganga Valley is called the Vedic Age because the four sacred *Vedas* (collections of Sanskrit hymns) were composed at this time. Gradually, the Aryans moved eastwards and settled down to practise sedentary agriculture. This meant the evolution of a more complex society and tribal republics developed, giving way to kingdoms.

It was the Vedic Age that gave birth to the social order known as the caste system. All traditional societies tend to be stratified; what makes the caste system peculiarly Indian is its accompanying code of ritual purity and pollution, elaborated to cover every aspect of human activity and life. In the beginning, the system was little more than a simple ordering of society into hierarchical divisions according to hereditary occupations. Actually, the order was never permanently fixed and groups moved up or down over periods of time. Castes have been known to coalesce and to splinter while some have disappeared altogether. Tribes drawn into the fold of Hindu society became castes, while some of the craftsmen's guilds that emerged in the medieval period began to intermarry and inter-dine exclusively and also evolved into hereditary *jatis*.

Since all the castes recognized themselves as making up parts of a whole, these social divisions did not mean that Hindu society was entirely fragmented. The exchange of goods and services between members of different castes, both within a village and beyond, led to mutual interdependence.

Brahmins, being the only class of Hindus who had access to the scriptures and could perform rituals, were accorded the highest status. By the 6th century, however, political developments made the ruling caste of Kshatriyas very powerful while commerce had become important and brought prosperity to the Vaishyas who were mainly traders. This meant these two groups were not willing to accept Brahminical superiority unquestioningly. Apart from this, other conditions also promoted the rise of new social and religious movements that threatened the established order. Society had grown more complex with sharper social distinctions. The cities that arose saw, for the first time, wealthy and ostentatious lifestyles and also abject poverty. A greater awareness of the ironies of the human condition made the old Hindu tradition of asceticism exert a profound influence on the several new sects that sprang up in the 6th century, of which Buddhism and Jainism were the most important.

Siddharta Gautama, later the Buddha or the Enlightened One, was born into a ruling Kshatriya clan of a republic in the foothills of the Himalayas. Declaring that the world was full of suffering whose root cause was desire, he founded one of the greatest religions of the world, based on the principles of non-violence and renunciation of worldly pursuits and pleasures. Buddhism was one of the major religions of India for over a thousand years. It grew to be an international faith, even as it disappeared in the land of its origin. Today, pilgrims from all over the world come to India to visit sacred places connected with the Buddha: Lumbini where he was born, Gaya where he meditated for 49 days before attaining Enlightenment, Sarnath (near Varanasi) where he preached his first sermons,

Kusinagara where he died, and other places where he lived and taught. Many scholars believe that the Buddha had never intended to found a new religion and did not see his doctrine as being distinct from the popular cults of his time, but rather as transcending them. In becoming a religion, Buddhism borrowed and adapted much from the popular beliefs of the time.

Its simple ritual was not based on sacrifice as Brahminical Hinduism was, but on the cult of *chaityas* or sacred spots. There were often small groves of trees or single trees and might also include tumuli, such as those where the ashes of revered ascetics had been buried. This form of worship was not only less expensive and more accessible but also appealed to 'simpler folk' who had retained many such pre-Aryan traditions of worship. Later, many of the famous Buddhist *viharas* (monasteries) and stupas arose on the same sacred spots.

The *stupa* began as an earthern burial mound which was revered by the local people. Later the *stupa* came to be particularly associated with Buddhism and the great Mauryan king, Ashoka, raised *stupas* all over India in the Buddha's honour. Excavations have shown that the existing *stupas* retain the character of the originals. They were large hemispherical domes, containing a small central chamber in which relics of the Buddha (distributed over various sites by Ashoka) were kept. The *stupa* was made of brick and then plastered over. It was surrounded by a railing which enclosed a path for ritual circumnambulation. Between the 2nd century BC and the 3rd century AD, the older *stupas* were greatly enlarged and beautified. The most famous are the Bharhut and Sanchi *stupas* in Madhya Pradesh and the Amravati limestone *stupa* in Andhra Pradesh. The first is famous for its sculpture, dated about 150 BC, of *yakshas* and *yakshis* (demi-gods and goddesses) and incidents from the Jataka tales.

The Sanchi *stupa* is celebrated for its four wonderful gateways and its railings. Each gateway consists of two square columns above which are three curved architraves supported by animals and dwarfs, the whole reaching some 34 feet in height. The *stupa* at Amravati, completed around 200 AD, was larger still and its carved panels tell the story of the life of the Buddha. It is interesting that when Sir Edwin Lutyens designed the Viceregal Lodge on top of the Raisina hill in New Delhi, he chose to top the sandstone building with a black dome reminiscent of the ancient *stupas*.

In the year 326 BC, Alexander the Great invaded India and was victorious in the Punjab until fear of mutiny among his troops forced him to return. The immediate effects of the invasion were not very important, though some Greek colonies were established in the north-west. It was the later Greeks who left a more lasting impact.

Of the states that arose in North India at the time of the Buddha, Magadha with its capital at Pataliputra (modern Patna) grew extremely powerful and easily vanquished its neighbouring rivals. Around the time of Alexander's invasion, the throne of Magadha was held by a king whom the Greeks called Sandrocottus, identified as Chandragupta, founder of the Mauryan line and architect of the greatest empire of Ancient India. The Mauryan administrative system was extremely elaborate and thoroughly systematized, and one of Chandragupta Maurya's advisers, Chanakya, wrote a Machiavellian treatise on statecraft and diplomacy (which much later won the author the honour of having New Delhi's present diplomatic enclave named after him).

Chandragupta Maurya's grandson, Ashoka, was one of the noblest and greatest rulers the world has known. He left a series of edicts carved on rocks and pillars scattered widely over the area that is present day India and also far beyond—as far as Kandahar in Afghanistan where his edict is in Greek, written in the Aramaic script. These are the oldest surviving written sources in ancient Indian history to have been deciphered.

Ashoka speaks of the remorse he suffered after a bloody victory against another state. The change of heart made him renounce violence and turn to the Buddhist faith. Accordingly, he adopted paternalistic policies at home and made peaceful overtures to other kings, including five Hellenic rulers. The traditional policy of conquest by war was replaced by what he called *dhamma--vijaya* or conquest through righteousness, while he preached *ahimsa* or non-injury to both men and animals.

Ashoka certainly played a very important role as a propagator of Buddhism, both within India and outside. It was he who sent a mission to Sri Lanka. By raising Buddhism to the level of a state religion, Ashoka gave it a great reach and power. The vast empire he inherited and added to in the early years of his reign did not last long after Ashoka's death, but the legacy of Ashoka is still an inspiring example. It is no coincidence that the republic of India has chosen the four-lion capital of the Ashokan pillar at Sarnath as its national emblem, and that the Ashoka wheel finds a place on the national flag.

The five centuries after the decline of the mighty Mauryan empire saw a series of invasions into India. The first invaders were the Greek of Bactria. Greek influences penetrated Indian culture, and and can clearly be seen in the sculpture of the Gandhara school, which produced many graceful statues of the Buddha. The style combines a Graeco-Roman aesthetic with spiritual values that are wholly indigenous.

At some time in the first half-century of the Christian era, a warrior tribe from Central Asia entered India and settled down to rule North India up to Varanasi in the East. They were the Kushanas—one of whom, Kanishka, played a crucial role in the spread of Buddhism to Central Asia and the Far East. It was really under the Kushanas that the Gandhara style reached its greatest heights and the school of Mathura sculpture developed. The Buddha image originated in this school, which was greatly influenced by Jain art but also partly inspired by some Greek motifs from the north-west. The material used is local sandstone and the style clearly evolved and acquired a greater quality of grace and spirituality over the centuries until it flowered into the Gupta style, which produced some of India's most beautiful sculpture.

In the 4th century, India saw the rise of another great empire under another Chandragupta. The line he founded is known as the Gupta line, and the Gupta period is acclaimed as the Golden Age of Ancient India. The reign of Chandragupta II, in particular, is a high watermark of the arts. One of the important sources for the history of this period is the account of a Chinese monk, Fa-hsien, a visitor to the Buddhist monastries and temples. The great Sanskrit dramatist Kalidasa lived and wrote at this time.

The earliest of the surviving free-standing Hindu temples date from the Gupta period. Before that, there was a tradition of rock-cut temples—artificial caves. Famous examples include the Barabar caves near Gaya, which are Mauryan, and the finest single example is the great *chaitya* hall at Karli (Western Deccan) carved in the beginning of the Christian era. Associated rock-cut monasteries developed along with the *chaitya* halls and, gradually, complexes of caves grew in size and number. The cave group at Ajanta in Maharasthra has 27 caves, dating from between the 2nd century BC and the 7th century AD. Although the splendid paintings on the walls have deteriorated with time, the colours are still clear and well contrasted. Originally, they must have been brilliant. The murals chiefly depict scenes from the Jataka tales and the life of the Buddha.

The later cave temples at Ellora, near Aurangabad (also in Maharashtra) are even more splendid. Between the 5th and 8th centuries, 34 caves were carved out. The greatest of these is the great Kailashnatha Temple of the Rashtrakutas. The entire rock face has been cut away and a splendid temple carved from the hillside—with a complex of rooms, gateway, pillars etc., all decorated with sculpture.

It was at this time that some of the finest religious art was produced. If the sculpture at Bharhut, Sanchi and Mathura is marked by sensuality, that of the Gupta age has a quality of serenity and spirituality—as exemplified in wonderful Buddhas of Sarnath, especially the image of the Enlightened One preaching his first sermon.

The Gupta Empire vanished by the middle of the 6th century, largely because of a series of invasions by the Huns or Hunas from central Asia. In the 7th century, the emperor Harsha was to restore some of the glories of the Guptas. He ruled most of North India, though by this time the structure of government can perhaps be best described as feudal and the age of the highly-centralized empire was over. The two important cities of the empire were Thaneshar and Kanauj. After Harsha, India saw a period of almost ceaseless warfare between rival dynasties.

The Tripartite Struggle

FOLLOWING THE reign of Harsha, his capital Kanauj came to be considered the symbol of of sovereignty over North India—a position to be acquired later by Delhi. For the contending empires that rose in India between the middle of the 8th century and the 10th century, control of Kanauj implied control of the upper Ganga valley; accordingly, much of the struggle between the Palas of Bengal, the Pratiharas of Rajasthan and the Rashtrakutas of the Deccan revolved around this city.

Although this period is remembered largely as being one of warfare, each of these three empires was able to establish a certain stability over a large territory and also to provide patronage to arts and letters.

In South India, from the middle of the 6th century, different lines—the Pallavas of Kanchi, the Chalukyas of Badami, the Pandyas of Madurai, the Cheras of Kerala—saw both hostilities and alliances amongst themselves.

Of them, the Pallavas were notable for their commercial and cultural ties with China and South-East Asia. Mostly Shaivite by faith, they built the famous shore temple at Mahabalipuram. Seventeen temples were carved from granite hills; today most of them have been washed into the sea, but the ruins are still spectacular. The founder of the Chola dynasty was originally a Pallava feudatory who captured Thanjavur. The Chola empire marks a high point in the history of South India. The Chola kings, having established their suzerainty over much of South India, conquered Sri Lanka and the Maldive Islands. Their victories were commemorated by the erection of Shiva and Vishnu temples at various places, the most important of these being the Rajarajeshwara temple at Thanjavur. The Chola empire declined in the early part of the 13th century and the Cholas were replaced by the Pandyas and the Hoysalas.

It is indicative of the wealth of the Cholas that they could build opulent cities such as Thanjavur, Kanchi and Gangai-kondacholapuram. It was at this time that the temple architecture of South India attained its climax. The rock-cut temples of the Pallavas were succeeded by structural temples in what is called the *Dravida* style. The style is characterized by the building of one storey above another, directly above the sanctum sanctorum. The number of storeys varied between five and seven and the superstructure was called the *vimanas*. A hall or *mandap* with elaborately carved pillars and a flat roof, in front of the sanctum sanctorum, functioned as a hall of audience and as the arena for the performances of the *devadasis* or temple dancers. Sometimes a passage was built around the sanctum to permit circumambulation by worshippers, and images of other gods were placed in this passage. This entire structure was situated in a walled courtyard with high ornate gates called *gopurams*. In time, the *vimanas* rose higher and higher, the *gopurams* grew increasingly elaborate and the number of courtyards increased to two or three. Thus, the temple became a miniature city with a number of permanent residents. The temples were supported by the income from lands granted to them and also from grants and lavish donations made by wealthy patrons. Soon, some temples were prosperous enough to venture into business themselves.

Sculpture also attained a remarkable standard during the same period, a monumental example being the giant 18 metre statue of Gomateshwara cut out of granite at Sravana Belgola. The 1,000-year-old statue depicts the Jain ascetic who meditated for so long that creepers grew and entwined themselves along his legs. The *Nataraja* or dancing Shiva figure attained classic perfection, especially when cast in bronze.

Religion

Buddhism and Jainism continued to decline (though the latter flourished in South India till the 10th century) while Hinduism saw a period of resurgence and expansion, expressed in the spread of the worship of Shiva and Vishnu. In eastern India, the *Shakti* cult became powerful. This entailed the worship of the female principle, in the form of a Hindu goddess. The later forms of Buddhism were influenced by *Shakti* elements and the cult of Tara, a Buddhist goddess, gained strength. Buddhism was gradually confined to eastern India. After the Palas, it lost royal patronage but, more significantly, the transformation of the religion made it indistinguishable from Hinduism. Jainism managed to retain a stronghold in western India under the patronage of the Chalukyas of Gujarat. Magnificent Jain temples, such as the Dilwara temple at Mount Abu, were built at this time.

In both North and South India the revival of Hinduism took two forms—the first being a renewal of faith in the Vedas and Vedic worship by a powerful literary and intellectual movement, and the second a parallel popular movement. In the north, this gained its impetus from Tantra while in the south the *bhakti* or devotional movement led by *Alwars* and *Nayanars*—popular saints and mystics—between the 7th and 12th centuries, won over many tribes whose tribal deities were gradually incorporated into the Hindu pantheon. *Bhakti* emphasized individual faith and worship and rejected the need for mediation between man and god by priests with their elaborate rituals and Sanskrit prayers.

Intellectually, the greatest contribution to Hindu philosophy was made by Shankara, in the 9th century. It is evident that his ideas aroused hostility from Buddhists and Jains. Shankara's philosophy of *advaita* denied any duality between God and the created world and declared that the apparent differences were only an illusion caused by ignorance. This philosophy is also called *Vedanta*. In the 11th century, Ramanuja tried to incorporate *bhakti* into the Vedic tradition and thus bridge the gap between the two movements in Hinduism. The tradition of Ramanuja was reinforced by a number of thinkers in both the north and the south so that, by the 16th century, *bhakti* was acceptable to all sections of Hindu society.

The Rajput States and the Turkish Conquest

I N THE 10TH century, a number of Rajput states arose in North India, bringing the Indian form of feudalism to its apogee. The basic unit of Rajput society was the clan, and the Rajput clans traced their descent variously from the sun and from the moon. They claimed the status of Kshatriyas, the warrior caste of the Vedas, and established themselves as the caste most suited to kingship. The more important ones included the Gahadavalas of Kanauj, the Paramaras of Malwa and the Chauhans of Ajmer. The Rajput rulers were in an almost constant state of war amongst themselves, which made it impossible for them to unite against a common threat when the Turks began their depredations.

This period (8th–12th century), the last stage of the Hindu ascendancy, saw a great flowering in temple architecture. The *nagara* style of temple became dominant. Its main feature was the tall, curved roof over the square sanctum or *garbhagriha*. An antechamber or *mandapa* led to the sanctum and sometimes the temple was surrounded by high walls with large gates. The finest examples in Khajuraho are the Parsvanatha, Vishwanatha and Kandariya Mahadeva temples, all built by the Chandellas, the Rajput rulers of the Bundelkhand region of central India. In Orissa, the most splendid temples are the Sun Temple at Konarak and the Lingaraja temple at Bhubaneshwar.

Many temples were built in other places such as Mathura, Banaras and Pushkar. However, as in the South, the later temples began to show an increasing tendency to elaborate ornamentation. In a sense, this was a reflection of the great wealth that some temples acquired. They were accepted as centres of social and cultural life and it was their wealth that made them attractive targets for. marauding armies from Central Asia, who were content to loot them and return with their spoils.

It was the Turkish adventurer Muhammed Ghuri of Ghazni who first looked to India for a direction in which to extend his power. Forced out of his Central Asian homeland by political events there, he conquered Delhi and eastern Rajasthan and established a base from which Turkish rule was extended over the Gangetic plain. Ghuri returned to Ghazni, leaving Indian affairs in the hands of his trusted slave, Qutb-ud-din Aibak, who consolidated and added to his master's gains. He later became the Sultan himself, severing the Central Asian connection and founding the independent Sultanate of Delhi. The dynasty founded by Aibak came to be known as the Slave Dynasty. The Slave Kings left behind some remarkable monuments, the most famous of which is the Qutb Minar in Delhi, built by Qutb-ud-din's successor Iltutmish.

The Mameluk or Slave Sultans introduced many Turkish elements into the arts of India and into statecraft, but the whole period of the Sultanate also saw the development of a new culture in North India, a synthesis of ideas brought in by the Turks and native traditions. This process of assimilation was accelerated under the later Sultans of Delhi. The Khaljis were the next important line and they were clearly of indigenous stock. The second Khalji Sultan, Ala-ud-din, extended the Sultanate of Delhi to embrace all of North India and also made some successful forays into the South. Significant Khalji monuments can be seen in the Delhi region. The fort of Siri, Ala-ud-din's capital, is now contained in a suburb of Delhi. As in most of the architecture of the Sultanate, Central Asian elements are here seen modified by the use of local materials and the traditions of local craftsmanship. Ala-ud-din built an arched gateway for the Qutb Minar. The Alai Darwaza, as it is called, testifies that the principles of the arch and the dome (which had originated in the Roman empire and travelled to Byzantium before being adopted all over the Islamic world) had also come to be incorporated in the lexicon of the Indian builder.

The Khaljis were replaced by the Tughlaqs and before the advent of the Mughals, it was probably the Tughlaqs who made the most significant architectural contributions in the area around Delhi. They built a new township called Tughlaqabad, which contains—amongst other monuments—the tomb of the founder of the line, Ghiyas-ud-din Tughlaq. Massive sloping walls are a characteristic of Tughlaq monuments which, like the flying buttresses of Gothic architecture in Europe, lend strength to the building. A later Tughlaq Sultan, Firoze Shah, however, tried to combine the arch with the older Indian tradition of lintel and beam. This can be seen both in his Kotla and in the Hauz Khas, his pleasure resort, which has arches on alternate storeys, with the lintel and beam used in between.

Tughlaqabad was abandoned soon after it was built and today it has a haunted quality. Tradition says it was cursed by the venerated Muslim saint and mystic Nizam-ud-din Auliya who declared it would become a wilderness where only herdsmen would wander. The next Tughlaq king was Mohammed bin Tughlaq who built a spectacular raised monument known as the Vijay Mandal (a peculiarly Sanskritized name, probably acquired in later years) which is now crowded in by a new South Delhi suburb but which must once have dominated the landscape with its series of connected arches. The Tughlaqs made greater use of greystone than of sandstone and since this stone does not lend itself to carving, Tughlaq buildings tend to be austere if grand.

Mohammed Tughlaq is perhaps the most controversial figure in the early medieval history of India. Cursed by a contemporary historian who declared him insane and—worse still—unorthodox, Mohammed Tughlaq in recent years has been rescued from this somewhat quixotic reputation and declared a visionary, a man born before his time. His famous 'mad' schemes, including the introduction of a token currency and the transfer of the capital to Central India, have been the subject of one of the most acclaimed plays in the modern Indian theatre.

There were no great Turkish Sultans after the Tughlaqs and the end of the 15th century saw the establishment of an Afghan line of kings—the Lodis. Afghan society was essentially tribal and the Lodi kings had to struggle to establish a more despotic form of government with centralised power vested in the king. Ultimately, the Lodis were defeated not so much by internal dissensions as by the invasions of the dynamic Central Asian Mughals led by Babur, himself dispossessed of his kingdom. Today, the Lodis are remembered by residents of Delhi who may stroll through the beautiful Lodi Gardens, where the tombs of the Lodi Kings are laid out. These stone buildings were once ornamented with coloured glazed tiles, predominantly in blue, but unfortunately the remains of this work are only fragmentary today.

The erosion of the highly-centralised nature of the Sultanate state gave many usurpers in the outlying parts of the kingdom the opportunity to assert their autonomy and many provincial kingdoms arose, as a result. Notable among these were the states of Jaunpur (in U.P.) under the Sharqi Sultans, Gujarat, Bengal, and Malwa in northern Madhya Pradesh. This political fragmentation had a beneficial side effect, in that it allowed the development of provincial styles of architecture.

The Sultans of Bengal built in a style which was distinct from the Delhi style, as the buildings in their capitals at Pandua and Gaur show. They made use of both stone and brick as materials and of the Bengal roof, which evoked the thatched roof of humbler dwellings in its upturned boat shape.

In Gujarat, the 15th century buildings of Ahmedabad drew from the rich heritage of Jain architecture and they are characterized by slender turrets, intricate carving and ornamental brackets. Fine examples of the Gujarat style are the Jama Masjid and the Tin Darwaza at Ahmedabad.

It was during the 15th century that the capital of Malwa was shifted to Mandu. The architecture of Mandu has an imposing quality, an effect that is heightened by the placing of the buildings on a high plinth. Coloured glazed tiles are used on a large scale. The more celebrated monuments of Mandu are the Jama Masjid, the Hindola Mahal and the Jahaz Mahal.

Meanwhile in the Rajput states, such as Mewar, the Hindu traditions of temple architecture and sculpture continued to flourish. The famous victory tower of Chittor was built at this time. In a highly religious age, places of worship were very important and at first the new rulers converted temples and other existing buildings into mosques. For example, the Quwwat-ul-Islam (might of Islam) mosque near the Qutb Minar in Delhi was originally a Jain temple that had been converted into a temple of Vishnu. In Ajmer, the *Arhai-din-ka-Jhonpra* ('the hut of two and a half days') is a mosque that was earlier a monastery.

Although the Turks used Hindu decorative motifs like the bell, the lotus and the swastika, they also introduced many new elements in design—geometric and floral patterns, interspersed with Quranic verses inscribed with calligraphic flourish. The traditional skill of Indian stonecutters found new channels. The walls of the small tomb of Iltutmish in Delhi are a splendid example of intricately carved stonework.

The Turkish Sultans brought to India elements of the highly sophisticated Arabo-Persian culture. In India the arts had also reached a high point in development and the wealth of these separate traditions led to an exchange of cultural ideas and the growth of what is called the composite Indo-Islamic culture.

Religious Ideas

The 15th and 16th centuries saw a remarkable development in religious ideas—the upsurge of the popular wave known as the *bhakti* movement. It was a movement of the common people, including those belonging to the lower castes. The *bhakti* tradition had already developed in the South but the principal reason for its wide appeal—the use of vernacular languages by teachers and mystics—also served to retard the spread of ideas to the North.

There was an old tradition of unorthodoxy in North India, the cult of *Tantra*, and so the mystics who preached brotherhood found a receptive audience. Kabir and Nanak were two popular saints who both attracted a number of followers. They denounced idolatry and other forms of ritual worship and also spoke of the meaninglessness of sectarian and caste distinctions. Ultimately, however, the followers of both banded themselves into different sects and, indeed, the followers of Nanak became a religious community—the Sikhs.

The non-sectarian stream within the *bhakti* movement was accompanied by the Vaishnava movement that centred around the worship of Rama and Krishna, two of the incarnations of the Hindu god Vishnu. The mystical poets, Chaitanya in Bengal and Meerabai in Rajasthan, reached great heights of fervour and literary expression in their exquisite lyric verse. There were other major saint-poets, too, whose poetry was humanist; it asserted the belief in individual worship and denied the need for a rigid apparatus of intervention between man and god. Ultimately, the caste system withstood all onslaughts, but the alienation of the lower castes was reduced and the rigours of the system were somewhat softened.

The Mughal Age

THE MUGHAL AGE of India, which lasted for three centuries, has become synonymous with grandeur and oriental opulence. The Mughals established a powerful polity that extended over the subcontinent, developed an elaborate administrative and military structure and created the climate for a tremendous flowering in the cultural fields: a wealth of ideas in philosophy and history as well as a new idiom in the arts.

The first Mughal ruler, Babur, was from Farghana, a small state in Trans-Oxiana. Driven from his homeland by the Uzbeks, he looked to the east for a prospective new empire. India, in the early 16th century, seemed the answer. The Lodi king's attempt to centralise power had alarmed both the Afghan chiefs—his countrymen—and the Rajput rulers, so that the invading army did not face resistance from anything like a united front. Babur was able to establish his control over North India in three crucial battles. Forced to fulfil his dreams of power in a strange land, Babur speaks nostalgically in his memoirs of the landscapes of his Central Asian homeland, especially of its gardens and streams. In India, Babur began the tradition of laying out formal gardens with running water. Examples of Mughal gardens that have survived include the Nishat Bagh and the Shalimar gardens in Kashmir. In fact, the Mughals extended the use of water channels into their palaces as a primitive 'air-conditioning' device. Babur was succeeded by his son, Humayun, whose rule was mainly a saga of struggle between the Mughals and the Afghans who were ably led by Sher Shah Suri. The latter actually ousted Humayun, and for 15 years ruled the most extensive empire since Mohammed

Tughlaq's. (It was Sher Shah who built the Grand Trunk Road, the 'river of life' of Kipling's *Kim*, which runs from Punjab to Bengal and is today named after the Afghan king.)

Sher Shah built a new capital on the bank of the Jamuna in Delhi, and the *Purana Qila* (Old Fort), with its magnificent ramparts and its handsome gates, testifies to the fertility of creative expression during the Afghan interregnum. Humayun was able to regain the throne of Delhi only after the death of Sher Shah in 1550, but his fatal fall cut short his reign. His favourite wife built him a superb mausoleum, not far from the old Fort. Humayun's tomb is a forerunner of the Taj Mahal. It is built in red sandstone, with detail work traced in marble and a large and elegantly proportioned marble dome. Raised on a plinth which itself has a series of arched doorways, the mausoleum makes use of many architectural features that later became characteristic of the Mughal style.

It was Humayun's son, Akbar, born to parents in exile, who consolidated the Mughal empire. He had to first eliminate diverse threats to his power—from the Afghan forces who had been waiting for an opportunity to recapture all of northern India, from powerful groups of ambitious nobles, and from rebellious rulers in the far-flung provinces. Akbar conquered Malwa, Gujarat and Bengal and brought much of Rajasthan under his own control. He negotiated a series of concordats with Rajput chieftains, some of which were cemented by matrimonial alliances. Only the state of Mewar refused to acquiesce. By allowing a fair degree of autonomy to the Rajputs, Akbar was able to convince them that the Mughal Empire did not threaten their own interests. Further, he inducted a number of the Rajput *rajas* into Mughal service.

Akbar's policy towards the Rajput states should be viewed not only as an example of his political maturity but against the background of his broad religious toleration that extended to all his subjects. His paternalistic and tolerant policy has been called *sulh-i-kul* or the belief in peace to all. He abolished the tax levied on non-Muslim subjects and the tax on Hindu pilgrimages.

An administrative genius, Akbar re-organized the system of assessment and collection of land revenue and also organized the nobility into a single structure that combined military, administrative and landholding functions. Because the Mughals are still associated with pomp and power, the personalities of the individual rulers have also become the stuff of legend and tradition so that now it is no longer easy to separate folklore from fact. Akbar, quite justly, is remembered for his tolerance and vision, his military and administrative genius and his patronage to scholarship and the arts. It is his son Jahangir who is fitted into a caricature—that of a uxorious drunkard.

It is true that Jahangir raised his father-in-law, Itmad-ud-daula, to the office of Chief Noble or Diwan and other members of the Empress Nur Jahan's family also benefited from the alliance, but it is not fair to say that Nur Jahan created a caucus that controlled all affairs of state. Until Jahangir's health failed, some eleven years after his marriage, he made all important political decisions. Nur Jahan's role was more that of a setter of fashions. She certainly played an important role in popularizing Persian art and culture at the court. It was when Jahangir's health broke down that she was catapulted into the political arena. This was, however, only part of the reason for the rebellion of her stepson Khurram, who later became the Emperor Shahjahan. He had his own ambitions and he was not the only Mughal prince who rebelled against his royal father. Jahangir had done so himself and it was a reflection of a basic weakness in Mughal polity that a successful prince frequently became a rival focus of power. This was largely because there was no clear tradition of succession among the Mughals.

Soon after Jahangir's death in 1627, Shahjahan managed to seize the throne. His reign saw great activity on many fronts, especially in the field of foreign policy. Today he is remembered by ordinary people for his magnificent monuments and the new city of Shahjahanabad that he built in Delhi.

The last years of Shahjahan's reign were marked by a bitter fratricidal war of succession among his sons. The ailing emperor nominated his son Dara as his heir, but Aurangzeb ultimately seized power and imprisoned his father who was kept captive in the Fort of Agra until his death eight long years later.

It is Aurangzeb's reign, indeed his very character, that has caused the most controversy among historians and laymen alike. He ruled for almost half a century and it was under him that the Mughal Empire attained the largest territory. Aurangzeb seems to have been a meticulous and hardworking ruler. He lived a life of austerity himself and sought to impose similarly spartan standards on his subjects. He forbade singing in the court and discontinued the practice of standing on a balcony to let the public see him (*jharoka darshan*) since he regarded this as unIslamic and superstitious. He banned astrology and would not consent to be weighed against gold and silver on special occasions.

Since Aurangzeb believed that the state was responsible for the moral welfare of subjects, he appointed officials whose duty was to see that citizens lived their lives in accordance with the *Sharia*. Aurangzeb banned the building of new temples but, in the early part of his reign, allowed old temples to be maintained. Later, in the face of rebellions from many quarters, he seems to have veered to the view that temples were centres of subversion because he ordered the destruction of several temples. Once this phase came to an end, Aurangzeb imposed the *Jizya*, the religious tax on non-Muslims which had been abolished by Akbar. This was undoubtedly a political measure meant to gain support from the orthodox Muslims, and it alienated a large section of the people. But on the whole, Aurangzeb's bigotry has been grossly exaggerated. He did no more than reassert the fundamentally Islamic character of the state. The number of Hindu nobles at the Mughal court continued to grow.

However, Aurangzeb's bumbling policy towards the Rajput princes undid the wise system worked out by Akbar and maintained by Jahangir and Shahjahan. So Aurangzeb lost the support of old allies in Rajasthan even while he had to face fresh rebellions in different parts of his empire. The protracted military campaign he conducted in the Deccan was a severe strain on imperial resources. Soon after Aurangzeb's death, the Mughal Empire began to decline rapidly.

Akbar was the first of his line to enjoy both the resources and the leisure to build on a large scale. He built a number of forts, including the famous Red Fort on the river Jamuna at Agra. The fort is enclosed by a high red sandstone wall from which it derives its name. It runs in the shape of a 'D', with the straight side along the river bank. Of Akbar's sandstone palaces in the fort, only one remains. The rest have been demolished, many of them by Shahjahan, who built in marble along the same riverfront.

Akbar built a new city at Sikri, near Agra, and gave it the name of Fatehpur ('the City of Victory') Sikri. It is built on top of a hill and contains a large artificial lake. Fatehpur Sikri contains many exquisite buildings, such as the Panch Mahal which consists of five pillared floors, each floor diminishing in size up to a small pavilion on top. It was built to house the harem and had finely carved stone screens to provide privacy. The Diwan-i-Khas or Hall of Private Audience appears, from the outside of the building, to have two storeys but inside it is one large, high room. In the middle stands a sturdy sandstone pillar that is extended by a cluster of carved beams modelled on a jewel casket.

Pietra dura was used on a large scale in the most famous of all Mughal monuments, the Taj Mahal in Agra. It was built by Shahjahan in memory of his beloved queen Mumtaz Mahal and is the culmination of the best of the Mughal traditions of architecture. Like Humayun's tomb in Delhi, it has a double dome. A smaller dome within a large one which is visible from the exterior allows for pleasing proportions from both within and without the building. Four minarets are positioned at four corners of the platform on which the building is raised. The marvellous restraint in the use of ornamentation creates an air of elegant understatement while the carved marble screens have a delicacy reminiscent of fine lace. The *chhatris* or kiosks that surround the central dome are themselves topped by small domes, while the use of the half-dome along the facade, at two levels, creates shadowy recesses that prevent any hint of monotony. The whole building is laid out in a formal garden in the Mughal style, and reflected in the waters of a pool in front of the mausoleum.

The Moti Masjid (Pearl Mosque) in the Agra Fort is also built entirely in marble while the Jama Masjid in Delhi in red sandstone. Both reflect the superb standard of design that had been reached under Shahjahan.

No less valuable was the Mughal contribution to the fine arts of miniature painting and jewellery. The Indian tradition of painting had been mainly that of illustrated palm-leaf manuscripts. Akbar's patronage was to provide the impetus for a vigorous revival. An imperial *karkhana* or atelier was set up in which artists from Persia as well as from many parts of India were included. Several books were illustrated—Persian as well as Indian. The *Akbar Nama* is one of the most celebrated illustrated texts. The original influences were indubitably Persian but India asserted herself soon, as Indian landscapes and scenes, with indigenous characters, animals and plants were depicted with increasing frequency. Soon Indian colours like peacock blue were also in use and the Mughal style developed an idiom that made it distinctive. The use of a rounded brush added an effect of depth that the somewhat flat Persian style had lacked. Portuguese missionaries at the court of Akbar introduced European techniques of perspective.

It was under Jahangir that miniature painting reached its greatest heights. Hunting scenes, battle scenes and scenes of the court continued to be painted, with interesting placements of individuals and groups of people. Portraits and paintings of animals also reached a level of great sophistication.

The failure of the later Mughals to provide enough patronage to painters caused them to disperse to different parts of the country and provincial styles of painting developed. The Rajasthani and Hill schools are examples of the regional styles that evolved. New themes such as the Radha-Krishna legend became popular subjects in these centres.

The Deccan

The Vijayanagara and Bahmani kingdoms dominated South Indian between the mid-14th and mid-16th centuries. Foreign travellers such as the Italian, Nicolo Conti, and the Persian, Abdur Razzaq, have left graphic accounts of the extravagant splendour of Vijayanagara (in Karnataka) and the ruins of the city still suggest the magnificence it must once have known.

By the end of the 15th century, the Bahmani kingdom was divided between the five independent states of Golconda, Bijapur, Ahmadnagar, Bidar and Berar. Of them, the first three were the most important in Deccan politics, until they were annexed by the Mughals in the 17th century. The presence of independent Islamic states in Southern India led to the development of a distinctive Deccani culture that, though profoundly influenced by trends in the north, also evolved its own separate characteristics. Nor were the influences transmitted in one direction only, for as the Deccan culture came of age, it was to stimulate the arts of the later Mughal.

The Sultan of Golconda constructed, among other buildings, the famous Char Minar in the new city of Hyderabad at the end of the 16th century. Its four high arches face four directions, while its four minars are four storeys high. In Bijapur, the most celebrated building is the Gol Gumbaz. Built in 1660, it has the largest single dome ever constructed.

Modern India

ALL THE INHERENT weaknesses of the monolithic Mughal state began to surface under the later Mughals, until a number of events in the eighteenth century reduced it to a mockery of what had been one of the mightiest empires in the world. Soon ambitious nobles began carving out independent principalities and the physical break-up of the empire began. In 1738-39, Nadir Shah of Persia invaded Delhi and looted the capital, carrying away the famous Kohinoor diamond and the jewel-encrusted Peacock Throne of Shahjahan, after a ghastly massacre of the citizens. He even took the Mughal Emperor as prisoner. Nadir Shah's invasion caused an irretrievable loss of prestige and laid bare the weakness of the empire to other Indian powers as well as to the European trading companies who had by now established footholds in parts of India—the Portuguese, the Dutch, the French and the English, all of whom had trading depots and wished to establish their rights to the exclusion of their rivals.

By the end of the 18th century the vast Mughal empire had shrunk to a few square miles around Delhi and, in 1803, Delhi itself was occupied by the British army.

The English East India Company soon became the most important of the foreign powers in India. It managed to eliminate its European rivals and, by actively intervening in local political affairs, to establish political sway over much of India. It was not hard to extract valuable privileges from the Mughal emperor and faced by any resistance, the Company did not hesitate to take recourse to arms. By 1765, the Company was the real ruler of Bengal and then began the period of what is called the Drain of Wealth, when the Company ceased to pay for Indian exports to England out of funds from home but financed its trade from revenues raised in India.

Over a relatively brief period, the British extended their hold to the south, the west, and indeed over all of India. Their military campaigns were also paid for from locally raised revenues. By the middle of the 19th century, a combination of direct annexation of territories with a system of alliance in which the Indian ruler became a mere figurehead in his own state made the British the rulers of all of India.

And then, in 1857, a mighty popular revolt broke out in northern and central India. Though it failed in the end, it showed that the people of India were not willing to be mute witnesses to the taking over of their land by what was indubitably a racist, exploitative, alien power. The revolt broke out originally among Indian sepoys in the British army but spread rapidly to peasants and artisans as well, classes which had suffered greatly from the British conquest and the colonial policies. When the revolt broke out, it spread quickly. The popularity of the rebels and their cause made the uprising hard to crush and the British had to wage a vigorous and ruthless campaign before they recaptured Delhi and took the last Mughal emperor prisoner.

In 1858, the last embers of the revolt had been stamped out and the governance of India moved from the Company to the Crown. Westminster Abbey had been playing an increasingly active role in Indian affairs over the last few decades, and now an Act of Parliament made this transfer of power absolute and overt. This year marks a watershed in colonial policy. The lessons of the Mutiny had been well learned. There was no further room for any vaguely liberal postures; from now on it was the age of aggressive and assertive imperialism.

As the high noon of imperialism approached, this surge of confidence found expression in grander and more ambitious buildings and monuments, until the climax of colonial architecture was reached with the Victoria Memorial in Calcutta. A massive marble tribute to the Queen-Empress, it attempts to combine European classical styles with self-consciously oriental touches. Today, it straddles the Maidan—luminous, impressive but utterly preposterous—a building with no declared utilitarian purpose, simply a monument to the Empire.

The same exuberant self-confidence is proclaimed by the neogothic grotesquerie of the Victoria Terminus building in Bombay. Highly ornate, with stone animals leaping out of its facade, it parodies the medieval cathedrals of Europe, reflecting the role the railways had come to play in the age of industry and empire.

The museums, marketplaces, secretariats and government houses of British India are now objects of nostalgia, but they rarely reflect much architectural imagination or innovation. The lasting contributions of the colonial builders have been more in the field of the smaller, less awe-inspiring structures—the dwelling-places and clubhouses that sheltered the sahib from India. The bungalow which was the nucleus for both was a purely Anglo-Indian phenomenon that evolved over two centuries—single-storeyed, with sheltered verandahs and at least one portico; the comfortable English country home, modified to suit the rigours of the Indian climate.

By the time Lutyens embarked on his ambitious project for the new capital city of New Delhi, however, the zest and vitality that characterize even the most bastardized 19th century structure had evaporated. The national movement was gathering force and as the rumblings grew closer, it was too late for arrogance, though too soon for regret. So that despite the stately situation on a hill, despite the magnificence of scale, despite the sweep of the vista, there is something a little wishy-washy about the token tributes to native styles—like the half-hearted concessions being made to the political demands of the nationalists.

Today many Indians justly regard the colonial buildings with a certain pride, and there are movements for their conservation in many cities. This is partly because they feel that the past cannot be simply blotted out and also because a new generation of Westernized Indians is distanced enough from the passions of the struggle for freedom to appreciate that the old monuments add to the colour and character of our cities.

It had been a somewhat similar realization—that there were lessons to be learnt from Western ideas—that moved a small but influential number of educated Indians in the 19th century to work for reforms in traditional society and religion. Discrimination on the basis of caste, the degradation of women, superstition—these were some of the issues that stirred intellectuals. By the end of the century, they were no longer isolated or without an audience. As the desire for reform was co-opted by larger, more popular movements, the idiom of reformist discourse changed from the strictly rationalist and largely secular language of the elite. But the seeds had been sowed, and it was ultimately as a reaction to Western ideas that the scriptures were re-read and many forms of injustice construed as aberrations and distortions of the 'real truths' revealed by ancient texts. The social, religious and cultural awakening of the 19th century with its emphasis on reform as well as its desire to rediscover the Indian heritage was to provide a background for the nascent nationalism that developed by the end of the century.

The year 1885, which marks the birth of the Indian National Congress, is viewed as the starting point of India's national movement. The early nationalists may not have achieved very much in concrete terms; it is true that they were not only few in number but essentially marginal, in the sense that they belonged to that small section of Indian society that had been exposed to Western ideas and education. All the same, this was a rich period of political development, for the nationalist arguments against the very basis of foreign rule were formulated at this time, by these very people. When larger numbers joined the struggle, it was their political and economic programme that was adopted and expanded.

In the 20th century, the National Movement began to widen its base, as more and more people were stirred by nationalist sentiment. The *Swadeshi* movement in 1905 saw a popular boycott of foreign goods, seen as both the symbols and the very essence of foreign domination. This more militant phase of the movement saw participation by women, students and members of different religious communities. The time was soon ripe, after the end of the First World War, for the advent of Mahatma Gandhi in Indian politics.

Mahatma Gandhi was responsible for making the struggle against imperial domination an all-India movement. Gandhiji not only drew people by his charisma but also knew how to channelize popular energy into political action. His visionary leadership brought together all sections of the Indian people—from the illiterate peasants and the Harijans or 'Untouchable' castes, hitherto alienated from mainstream politics, to the middle classes and the privileged, who often sacrificed personal benefits for the nationalist cause.

Gandhiji's method of non-violent agitation is justly celebrated. He was already in his mid-forties when he came to India from South Africa, but he brought with him experience of agitation against an oppressive government, a set of new ideas on the nature and methods of struggle itself and, most important, a wonderful capacity to place his finger on the pulse of popular emotion. In a few years, he had understood the Indian situation and the needs and aspirations of the people as no one had before him. He tried out some of his ideas by organizing small *satyagrahas* (struggles for righteousness) over specific issues in different before trying to organize agitations on a national scale. In 1919, he called for a *satyagraha* against repressive laws in Punjab and it was at a public meeting called in the course of this movement that the infamous incident at Jalianwala Bagh, took place, when a peaceful crowd was fired upon by British troops, resulting in a large scale carnage.

In 1921, Gandhiji called for a national agitation—non-violent non-cooperation with foreign rule was the method—in keeping with the Gandhian philosophy of the impossibility of divorcing means and ends. The movement evoked an overwhelming response all over India but, true to his principles, Gandhiji did not hesitate to call off the agitation at the height of its power when a violent incident broke out.

The second major agitation, launched in 1931 by Gandhiji's famous march against the imposition of tax on common salt, excited an even greater fervour. By the end of World War II it was clear to the British that they could not rule a people against their will. At the stroke of midnight on August 15th, 1947, India became a free nation.

Tradition and Modernity

INDIA AS A sovereign nation has remained something of an enigma to observers and scholars. Cassandras had predicted that the country would splinter, become another third-rate dictatorship, sell out to one or other of the Super Powers. But, scarred as the republic was at birth by the trauma of partition into two countries, India managed to survive—and develop.

India is one of the few countries that have disproved the assertion that democracy and underdevelopment cannot co-exist. Time and time again, the Indian electorate has proved that it is aware of its power. Cynics are quick to point out that considerations of caste, region and community have provided axes for political mobilization and support. What they fail to notice is that through this process, traditional loyalties and institutions are themselves transformed. The structures may be conservative but the content and the demands are new, and through them the old forms are themselves meta-morphosed.

To wish away the many impediments and constraints that make democracy difficult would be naive. They were kept in mind by the country's Founding Fathers who produced one of the lengthiest and most comprehensive written constitutions in the world. To India's first Prime Minister, Jawaharlal Nehru, must go the credit for having the vision to evolve an imaginative foreign policy that was to prove pathbreaking. India's refusal to align with either of the world's political blocs as they emerged after the Second World War became the nucleus of an international movement. With Presidents Tito of Yugoslavia and Nasser of Egypt, Nehru blazed the trail for a growing number of newly-emergent nations who became independent in the decolonization era following the War.

The same refusal to be drawn into relations of dependence has characterized India's economic policy since 1947. And India's economic development has, like her political growth, bemused commentators and academics. In terms of National Product and per capita income, the rate of growth has been small enough to earn the derisive epithet, the 'Hindu rate of growth'. Yet India's principal aim was self-reliance and, with this end in mind, the state planned to develop a solid core of basic and heavy industries. Today India has an impressive heavy engineering base, produces its own steel, and builds its own ships as well as many of its aircraft. The progress in agriculture is equally impressive. After centuries of recurrent famines, India is finally independent of the vagaries of the monsoons. Even in years of drought, famine no longer stalks the country because the Green Revolutions in wheat and rice have made it possible to maintain stocks of excess foodgrains from the bumper harvests.

Indians are not unaware of the hazards of rapid 'modernization'. Apart from the far-reaching changes that are transforming the traditional bastions of Indian society—caste, the joint family and the village community, industrialization and commerce have not developed without hazard.

The villagers of Chapora in northern Goa are up in arms against a move to 'develop' their area as a tourist resort by the sea. They feel, quite reasonably, that building activity will endanger the local fort. The fort was built early in the 18th century and is a source of pride to the villagers. Their intuitive sense of history has spearheaded the conservation movement in the area. Today much of India faces the same dilemma as the people of Chapora. How does one reconcile the compulsions of 'progress' with an awareness of the past, especially when the two seem to conflict? More than ever before, Indians are aware of the need to grow and develop as a modern nation. Yet they also realize that they are fortunate to possess traditions in the arts, architecture, natural wealth and lifestyle that are still very much alive and vibrant.

Today the wildlife of India is recognized to be as much a part of the national heritage as the Taj Mahal. The English word *jungle* is Indian in origin and, indeed, there was a time when even the vast cultivated plain of the Ganga was covered with dense forests. There is much public concern about the preservation of the remaining tracts of jungle. These are not only beautiful in themselves, with their variety of trees and plants, but are the home of animals and birds of a wild beauty.

In the foothills of the Himalayas is the Corbett National Park. This is the area where the famous naturalist and killer of man-eating tigers and leopards first became famous and it is only fitting that India's first National Park was named after him. The Ramganga river, bordered by *shisham* trees, flows through the park. The river valley is the grassy home of *chitals*, hog deer, and some swamp deer. There are isolated clumps of vividly flowering trees in the predominantly *sal* forest. The park is noted also for its *sambar*, barking deer, pig, *langur*, red jungle fowl and for tigers. Other parks noted for tigers include the Kanha National Park in Madhya Pradesh, the sanctuaries in the Sunderbans, West Bengal, and Rewa, Madhya Pradesh.

The Bandipur sanctuary near Mysore is on a rocky plateau with a picturesque landscape dotted with stunted trees. It is famous for the *gaur* or Indian bison, just as Periyar in Kerala is celebrated for its wild elephants. A part of the river Periyar has been dammed to form is an artificial lake set in wooded hills, and is reckoned to be one of the most spectacular reserves in India.

The Gir forest in Gujarat is the last resort of the Indian lion. The Rann of Kutch is the home of the wild ass and in the beautiful mountains of Kashmir is found the *barasingha* or Kashmir stag. In the Brahmaputra Valley is Kaziranga, covered with thick grass and jungle—the habitat of the Indian rhino.

For bird-lovers, there are a number of colonies of breeding water birds in India, the most famous of which is the Ghana bird sanctuary near Bharatpur in Rajasthan. Here you can spy the white ibis, the moorhen, the purple coot, the dabchick, the pheasant-tailed jacana, the magnificent painted stork and many, many more—including the Sarus cranes that pair for life and have become in India symbols of a happy marriage.

Crafts

It is easy, while recounting the past glories of India's wealth of art and architecture, to imagine the country as a vast museum full of antiquities and beautiful objects created many centuries ago. In fact, the crafts of India are a living tradition—not mass-produced replicas of museum pieces, but objects of beauty and utility made by hand—whether luxurious items such as finely inlaid pieces of gold jewellery from Jaipur or humbler images of gods and goddessess woven from dyed straw by village women in North Bihar.

Today there is a greater awareness of the aesthetic quality of things of everyday use—simple toys, ritual objects and decorative designs created not for the collector or the connoisseur but fitting, instead, into the daily round of domestic work and worship. Many of the tribal crafts fit into this category. In Bastar, a district of Madhya Pradesh with a predominantly tribal population, bell metal is moulded into stylized figurines by the *cire perdue* process. It is interesting to observe that one of the finds excavated at an Indus Valley site is a similarly-made figure of a dancing girl.

The celebrated Bankura horse chosen by the Central Cottage Industries Emporium as its symbol was originally made in Bankura, West Bengal, for symbolic sacrifices. The elegantly disproportionate long neck of the terracotta horse was to facilitate ritual decapitation. Votive offerings are spread on the embroidered cloths or *rumals* of Chambal, Himachal Pradesh. Many of these examples of folk art have now been 'discovered' and are produced for the market, but a wealth remains unknown to the curio shops of the big cities.

The textiles of India were one of the main attractions that drew the European traders to her coast and there is still a dazzling array of weaves and designs produced by weavers on looms operated by hand.

Cotton, silk and—to a much lesser degree—wool are the traditional fabrics of India. Silk was regarded as the 'purest' textile, favoured for occasions of religious and ritual importance. The two greatest centres of silk-weaving are both important places of Hindu pilgrimage—Banaras in North India and Kanjivaram in the South.

Silk fabrics are now printed in many parts of India, but Kashmir and Bengal have been major centres of block printing for a long time. Tussore or raw silk is produced and printed or woven with designs in different centres. The Kosa silk of Madhya Pradesh is a fine example.

It is in cotton, some would argue, that the Indian weaver really extends himself to produce the most dazzling variety of colours and designs. Important centres of cotton weaving are widely distributed over the country.

In Rajasthan and Gujarat, the fine art of *bandhani* (tie and dye) has been perfected. The two states are also important centres for printed textiles and, usually, the hand block is employed. The *kalamkari* cloths of Andhra Pradesh are dyed after designs are painted on in hot wax. The designs are frequently arabesques, with much use of entwining vines and stylized birds, poppies and pomegranates while the colours are typical of vegetable dyes—indigo, madder red, olive green, dusty pink and brown.

In the range of woven cotton textiles, there is a multitude of weaves that makes enumeration difficult. Chanderis from Madhya Pradesh, Dhonekhalis and Tangails from Bengal, Venkatagiris from Andhra Pradesh—the array is startlingly varied. The *ikat* weavers of Orissa and Andhra also produce cotton textiles, while young designers are infusing new ideas into the traditions of many centres.

Finally, there is a range of embroidered textiles from the celebrated *chikan* work of Lucknow to the crewel stitch work on wool done in Kashmir and the densely worked cloths of Kutch, which often include mirror-work.

In wool, there is the tradition of very fine embroidery in Kashmir, weaving in Kulu (Himachal Pradesh), Almora (Uttar Pradesh) and in many parts of the North East. The fabric itself can range from coarse wool wastes in Rajasthan to the extremely soft, light and warm *pashminas* of Kashmir.

Fine jewellery in precious metals, chiefly gold, has been crafted in India for centuries. Notable among the multitude of designs and styles is the *meenakari* work of Rajasthan where gold jewellery is enamelled in vibrant colours. This work is done in silver as well and, increasingly, goldsmiths are turning to silver as the preferred base. Rajasthan, Delhi, Agra and Orissa are among the old homes of silverware, the last specializing in fine filigree work.

In Thanjavur, Tamilnadu, ornate copper plates are embossed with silver, while the bronze statues of the dancing Shiva, also from the South, are justly famous. Brass is used to make the heavy oil-lamps essential for many rituals and also many vessels and utensils of daily use. In Moradabad, Uttar Pradesh, and Jaipur, Rajasthan, coloured inlay work on brass is an important industry. The designs are traced on brass, then filled in with coloured lacquer and polished. A distinctive handicraft of Bidar in Andhra Pradesh is Bidriwork—gun-metal inlaid with fine floral or geometric designs in silver. Damascene work with gold or silver wire ornamentation on brass transforms items of household use like betelnut cutters.

An expensive material that is the medium for some very fine carving is ivory. Delhi, Agra and Kerala have been centres of ivory work for centuries while in much of the South, heavy rosewood furniture was sometimes decorated with fine ivory inlay.

There is a vast and varied selection of crafts in a diversity of materials and mediums—from the delicate glazed blue pottery of Jaipur to the vibrant Madhubani paintings, once used to decorate mud walls in Bihar villages but now done on paper for the market.

Festivals and Fairs

Indians are a devout people and all the major festivals have a religious hue, though it is possible to detect an underlying unity with nature that links the major occasions for communal celebration with the solar and lunar calendar, with seasons and harvests. Many of the festivals that are observed today go back to tribal and pre-Aryan ways of life. In India's predominantly agricultural society, many festivals are clustered around the months of October and November, when the gains from the summer crop are lavished on revelry and ritual. In western India, the important festival of Ganesh Chaturthi is marked by large processions in honour of the elephant-headed god, worshipped as the remover of all obstacles, while in the southern state of Kerala, Onam is observed with colourful boat races.

In most parts of India, ten days of jubilation reach their climax on Dassehra with the ceremonial incineration of huge effigies of Ravana, the evil king of Lanka vanquished by the righteous Rama. This legendary battle is the subject of the great epic, the *Ramayana*, and the story is enacted over several evenings in the *Ramalila*, a spectacular combination of music, dance, mime and theatre. Of all the *Ramalilas*, that of Ramnagar in Banaras is the most famous.

At the same time, Bengal celebrates Durga Puja—also a festival that marks the triumph of good forces over evil. Images of the mother goddess, Durga, who killed a buffalo-riding demon called Mahishasura, are worshipped over several days and then ritually immersed in the nearest body of water—river, lake or pond. Also called *Navaratri* or the festival of nine nights, it is celebrated variously in different parts of the country, but the telling of *kathas* or divine stories is a widespread feature. In Gujarat, the traditional *garba* dance, with the rhythmic clapping of short wooden sticks, is performed around earthen oil-lamps.

Soon after Dassehra comes the festival of lights, Diwali, to mark the return of the victorious Rama to his capital. Every house is decorated with small oil-lamps (now increasingly replaced by wax candles or electric bulbs) seen by many as symbols of spiritual illumination, and fireworks are let off. This is also the occasion to worship Lakshmi, goddess of prosperity and well-being. For traders, Diwali marks the end of the old financial year when new accounts books are opened.

On all these occasions, religious fervour is rivalled and sometimes overshadowed by festivities and jubilation, but in the spring festival of Holi the religious aspect is almost completely subsumed by revelry that can best be compared to the Carnival. Originally a fertility festival of ancient origin, Holi is the festival of colour; people sprinkle coloured water and powder on one another. A mildly intoxicating drink made from the cannabis plant is drunk and an atmosphere of abandon builds up. There is a tradition of special songs sung only during Holi, which has come to be associated with the legend of Krishna, the cowherd god of Vrindavan.

There is a host of lesser, local feasts and festivals such as Teej which is observed only in North India and is a women's festival. It is celebrated during the rainy season. Women in groups dye the palms of their hands with intricate designs in henna and sing seasonal songs, often on swings.

The famous chariot festival of Orissa has given a word to the English language—'juggernaut'. This is the occasion for the ceremonial chariot-ride of Lord Jagannath which draws pilgrims to Puri. In the past, ardent devotees would sometimes fling themselves under the chariot wheels in their fervour.

Festivals in India are primarily religious, and different communities—Christian, Muslim, Zoroastrian, Jain and Sikh—observe diverse holy days. Even for the non-believer, every festival is an occasion to remember—not only for its colour and spectacle, but also for the uplifting experience of seeing a faith expressed and re-affirmed. The vast *melas* or fairs are the most inspiring to observe as thousands of people travel miles to take ritual dips in ponds and in the sacred waters of the Ganga. Yes, inevitably we return to the Ganga, which courses its way through the hearts of millions in India. There are other *melas*, of course, and many of them are both important and popular. The Pushkar *mela* held every November near Ajmer, for example, draws pilgrims and, inevitably, sellers of crafts, to the famous lake near the only important Brahma temple of India. At the Sonpur Mela in Bihar, brisk trading in cattle and livestock is done in tents that spring up on the river bank on the auspicious full moon night (Purnima) in the month of Kartik (October-November). And there is the vast *mela* at Gangasagar, where the Ganga finally merges into the sea, held every year after the harvest in the winter month of Pausha when the sun enters the sign of Capricorn. But, ultimately, few *melas* can compare to the great Kumbha Mela at Prayag, near Allahabad, where the Ganga, the Jamuna and the mythical Saraswati, named for the goddess of learning and the arts—merge and flow on as one. Held every twelve years, the Kumbha Mela draws pilgrims from all corners of the country who walk miles and stand for hours in the cold water at sunrise in the North Indian winter, knowing only they are blessed to be able to do so—for who knows what will happen by the next Kumbha. . . .

On your journey through India you will encounter many faces, many things. From the jungles of the *terai*, Jim Corbett country, to the dense city of Calcutta, from the highly-skilled master craftsman who weaves finely-knotted Kashmiri carpets to the potter who churns out cheap throw-away clay pots to drink tea in—many levels coexist in India and you will have to make your choice, your own discovery, as you embark on a voyage that covers both space and time.

Illustrations

An annual pageant of sound and colour is the ceremony of Beating the Retreat, where massed bands from the Armed Forces perform in the arena created by Lutyens—the Vijay Chowk (Victory Square) before the Rashtrapati Bhavan (Presidential Palace).

The 12th century Qutb complex was created by the Turkish dynasty which ushered in the era of Islamic dominance. The 73 metre high Qutb Minar is named after a Sufi mystic, Qutb-ud-din Bakhtiar Kaki.

Congregational prayers in the Jama Masjid are held to mark the festival of Id which concludes the forty-day Ramzan—a period of prayer and abstinence. The great 17th century mosque was built by the Mughal emperor Shahjahan.

Above: A glimpse of Shahjahan's Red Fort through the crowded thoroughfares of Chandi Chowk, one of the oldest and busiest markets of Delhi. *Below*: Within the Red Fort, the emperor's Hall of Private Audience from where he conducted matters of state.

Above: The remnants of the Purana Qila, citadel of the second Mughal emperor Humayun. *Below*: The tomb of Humayun, father of the great Akbar. One of the earliest examples of the Mughal tomb and garden complex, it is in many of its features a forerunner of the Taj Mahal.

The Taj Mahal in its formal and strictly symmetrical garden setting. Built in the 17th century by Shahjahan to commemorate his beloved empress Mumtaz Mahal, the marble mausoleum is reckoned to be one of the wonders of the world.

Left: The cenotaphs of Shahjahan and his consort under the dome of the Taj. The emperor's grave lies off-centre, the only asymmetrical detail in an otherwise perfect architectural composition. *Right*: miniatures of the imperial couple on ivory (courtesy of the Archaeological Survey of India, New Delhi).

The Taj is wonderfully designed to be experienced from all sides and distances. Here, in a morning mist across the river Jamuna, it appears as a cluster of dreaming domes and minarets.

The combination of elemental water and sky with marble sculpted into domes, cupolas, alcoves and minarets creates an aura of mystery and enchantment.

Views of the Taj Mahal from the air, showing the tomb's uncannily skilful siting on a bend in the river Jamuna. This master-stroke has enabled the Taj to be viewed from miles away.

Aerial views of Akbar's capital at Fatehpur Sikri (*above*) and Agra Fort (*below*). Both were built by Shahjahan's grandfather, Akbar the Great, but most of the structures in the Fort were altered and rebuilt in marble by Shahjahan.

Above: The Khas Mahal in the Agra Fort where the deposed emperor Shahjahan spent his last years, gazing from his marble prison at the Taj Mahal glistening in the distance. *Below*: Entrance pavilion of the Samman Burj, built by Shahjahan in the Agra Fort. The walls and pillars of the structure are beautifully inlaid.

40

Above: The tomb of Itimad-ud-daula, built in 1628 by his daughter, the empress Nur Jahan. The fine detail of marble work is akin to that of the Taj. *Below*: The tomb of the Sufi saint Shaikh Salim Chisti, built in 1572 by Akbar. Sikri was chosen as the site for Fatehpur in homage to the mystic.

The desert in Jaisalmer. Although much of western Rajasthan is made up of sand dunes and scrub, the trade routes plied by camel caravans brought much wealth to the wilderness.

Jaisalmer Fort, built in the 12th century by the Bhatti chieftain Jaisal. The citadel, a triumph of architectural aesthetics, appears to have grown out of the hill and been moulded by the elements.

The Hawa Mahal near the Jaipur City Palace is a fascinating conglomeration of casements piled five storeys high. It is thought to have been a look-out pavilion for the strictly segregated palace ladies.

Views of the Jaipur City Palace, built in the early 18th century by the extraordinary king Jai Singh II. He was not only a town planner and architect of vision but a brilliant soldier, historian and man of science.

Inside the Phool Mahal (Flower Palace), part of the Jodhpur royal complex. The palaces of Jodhpur Fort exhibit a skilful blending of traditional Indian decoration and European baroque elements.

47

Most Hindu homes in Rajasthan have a shrine dedicated to one or more gods of the pantheon. Here is an elaborate polychromatic Ganesh (the elephant-headed god of propitious beginnings) in the courtyard of a house in Udaipur.

Ritual bathing in the Pushkar Lake during the Kartik Purnima or autumn full moon. At night devotees conclude the rites of worship by setting hundreds of oil lamps afloat in the waters of the lake.

The Amber Palace with Jaigarh Fort in the background. The entire complex was built between the 12th and 18th centuries in a style which gracefully blends Islamic and native Rajput elements.

50

The 17th century Jag Mandir on Pichola Lake is one of the beautiful island palaces of Udaipur. The youthful Mughal prince Khurram who later became Shahjahan lived here in exile after rebelling against his imperial father Jahangir.

Monastery in Ladakh, the northernmost district of the scenic state of Jammu & Kashmir. This magnificent high cold desert area is where the Tibetan form of Buddhism most strongly survives today.

Buddhism has been for centuries a powerful force in the Himalayan belt, and continues to be nurtured in the monasteries of the region. The exiled Dalai Lama, spiritual leader of the Tibetan Buddhists now settled in India, conducting a ceremony with a group of monks.

A Buddhist *thang-ka* or cloth painting from a monastery in Ladakh, depicting Shaiye, the ruler of the Dead, holding the universe in his grip. Yogic practices are part of Mahayana Buddhism and entail meditation centred on a complex geometrical design called a *mandala*.

The lush valley of Kashmir has for centuries been a cool haven for those seeking respite from the scorching heat of the plains. Its lakes, high grassy pastures and vistas of snow have earned Kashmir the epithet of the Switzerland of Asia.

Above: Moonlight silvers the peaks, forests and streams of Pahalgam, the valley of the shepherds. *Below*: The Dal Lake in Srinagar, with one of its many floating islands—Char Chinar, named for its four ancient *chinar* trees.

The lakes of Kashmir are plied by little quicksilver boats known as *shikaras*, which expertly ferry goods and passengers across the waterways.

The two symbols of Kashmir—the *chinar* leaf and the *shikara*—caught in a moment of stillness at dawn before the bustle of daily activity takes over life on the lake.

Sunrise on the river Ganga in the city of Varanasi, sacred to the Hindus. The day begins early on the ghats, as a dip in the river at sunrise is considered auspicious and purifying.

Benaras has fifty-two ghats, some for ritual bathing and some for cremation. The waters of the river Ganga are considered by devout Hindus to be the elixir of salvation, endowed with the power to cleanse the souls of those who bathe in it and liberate those whose ashes are immersed in it from the cycle of rebirth.

66

Woven bamboo umbrellas shield the *ghatias,* the priests who officiate in the various rituals of river worship.

The Brahma ghat (*above*) and the Manikarnika ghat (*below*). The history of Banaras can be traced back 4000 years, and most of the existing ghats date back to at least the 18th century.

Above; The Ahilyabai ghat (*left*) and the Viswanath temple (*right*). The roof of the latter was plated with about 850 kilograms of gold by the Sikh Maharaja Ranjit Singh in 1839. *Below*: Two Buddhist places of pilgrimage near Banaras—the Dhamek Stupa at Sarnath (*left*), the site of Buddha's first sermon, and the nearby Mulagandhakuti Vihar (*right*) where he used to meditate.

The explicit treatment of eroticism in the Khajuraho temple sculptures is probably rooted in Tantrism. This system holds that the ritual union of male and female holds the key to the dissolution of the Self in the Ultimate Reality.

Ornate sculptural decoration is a feature of the temples dating from the last great flowering of Hindu religious architecture (8th-12th century AD). Of the original 85 temples in the Khajuraho complex, 20 survive today.

71

The Victoria Memorial in Calcutta, a relic of the high noon of the British empire in India. This marble tribute to the Queen-Empress Victoria combines European classical styles with self-consciously oriental touches.

The Howrah Bridge in Calcutta, once the capital of British India and still the most populous city of the sub-continent. Despite its many problems, Calcutta has retained much of its character as the intellectual and cultural capital of modern India.

The famous 13th century temple at Konarak dedicated to the Sun God. It has been conceived as Surya's chariot, with twelve wheels and seven rearing horses—a supreme achievement of the creative imagination and sculptural realization.

Vignettes from the Sun Temple. *Above*: Female musicians (*left*) sculpted larger than life on the roof of the porch and (*right*) carved in relief on the outer panels. *Below*: Details of the ornamentation on the chariot wheel (*left*), and (*right*), the benignly smiling image of Surya framed by a flaming arch.

Odissi is the lyrical temple dance of Orissa, once performed in rituals centered around Lord Jagannath, an incarnation of Vishnu. Here the dancer holds a stance beneath the richly sculpted gateway (*torana*) of the Muktesvara temple.

The Rath Yatra or Car Festival in Puri has been a major annual event in Orissa for almost ten centuries. Wooden carved images of deities belonging to the local cult of Jagannath are placed on great chariots and drawn in procession by thousands of ecstatic devotees.

Fishing catamarans in the sunset. Orissa has an ancient tradition of seafaring and a long and scenic coastline, in parts of which the sea recedes by as much as five kilometers at low tide.

Above and *opposite*: Religious devotion is a living principle of everday life in Orissa, where the humblest Hindu shrine is tended as lovingly as the great temples in which the state abounds.

The famous bas-relief depicting the descent of the Ganga at the Mahabalipuram temple complex. A natural cleft in the rock has been imaginatively used to portray the river, around which divinities, sages and animals cluster in homage.

Above: The Meenakshi temple complex in Madurai, built in the Dravida style with towering polychromatic *vimanas. Below:* A view of the interior, showing the main hall or *mandap* in front of the sanctum sanctorum.

Above: The 17.5 metre high monolithic, free-standing stone image of the Jain saint Gomatesvara at Shravana Belgola near Mysore. *Below:* Sunset on the southernmost tip of India, Kanya Kumari.

The elephant-headed Ganesha, son of Shiva and Parvati, widely worshipped as the god of wisdom and the remover of obstacles. Hindus launch most enterprises with an invocation to this deity.

Kartikeya, also known as Skanda, is the younger brother of Ganesha and a favourite deity in South India. He is variously depicted as an enchanting little boy or a haughty young warlord, and his mount is the peacock Paravani.

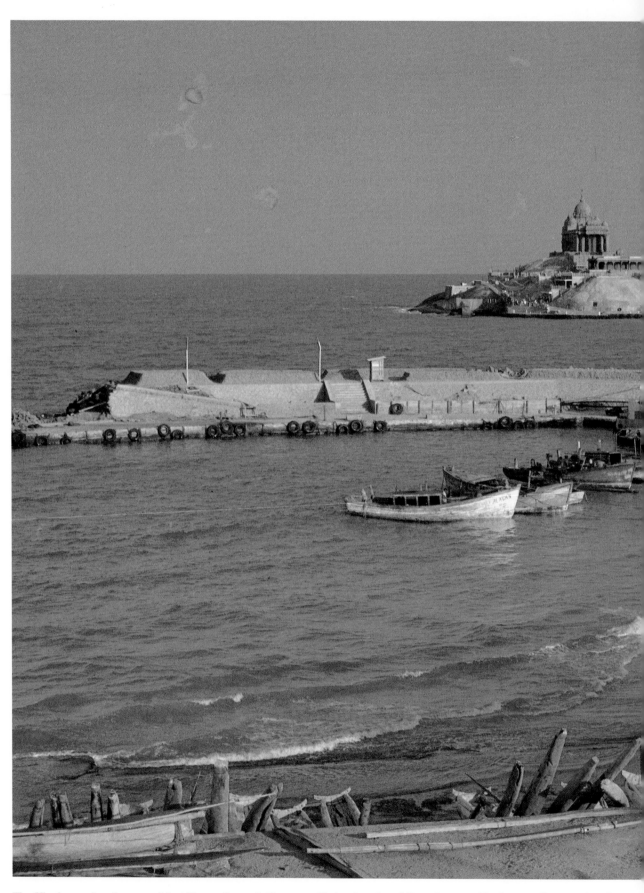

The Vivekanand rock memorial at Kanya Kumari. The great Vedantic saint-philosopher would often meditate at the site where three oceans meet—the Arabian Sea, the Bay of Bengal and the Indian Ocean.

The 16th century Char Minar, built by the Sultan of Golconda in the heart of the city of Hyderabad. Its four arched portals face in four directions, while its four minars are each four storeys high.

Bibi-ka-Makbara, the tomb of the Mughal emperor Aurangzeb's consort Dilras Banu. Built in the city of Aurangabad, it resembles in shape and design the Taj Mahal built by Aurangzeb's father Shahjahan.

Goa has an almost uninterrupted 105 km long coastline. Of its forty-odd beaches, the most popular and well developed are the contiguous Calangute-Baga-Anjuna beaches.

Through its history of five millenia, India has played host to a multitude of peoples and cultures. Those who remained were effortlessly accommodated into the Indian kaleidoscope. And to this day, few can journey through India without discovering some vital part of themselves as well.

96